Legend

1000 MIGLIA 1955,
victory of Sir Stirling Moss driving
a Mercedes 300 SLR

STIRLING MOSS 80/80

FOREWORD

It gives me enormous pleasure to be asked to write a few words in recognition of the huge contribution that Sir Stirling Moss has made to motor sport. I first met Stirling at one of my Grandfather's Easter cocktail parties in the Long Hall at Goodwood House. He always invited the drivers to a party during the Easter weekend and, although I was very young, I well remember being formally introduced to the famous Stirling Moss and getting his signature in my autograph book. I can see it now, crystal clear, a tiny squiggle sitting all on its own in the middle of a clean white page. The most treasured entry in the most treasured possession of a car mad six year old. When we started the Festival of Speed in 1993 it seemed absolutely natural that I should invite Stirling to be one of our founding Patrons. He has since played an important and enthusiastic role in the success of both the Festival and the Revival.

The name of Stirling Moss is of course inexorably linked with Goodwood Motor Circuit where he had his first and last race. Amazingly, he won that first ever race and he went on to win all the major prizes of that era including the Tourist Trophy and the World Sportscar Championship with Aston Martin. In my opinion he is the greatest racing driver in the history of the sport. No other driver has so successfully embraced so many different disciplines. Stirling always says that his hero, and Mercedes team-mate, Juan Manuel Fangio was a faster driver but there are many who would put these two legends on the top step together.

Even now, in his 80th year, Stirling is as energetic and enthusiastic as ever, getting back behind the wheel of many of the great cars that he used to race in anger. To this day many people come to our Revival weekend just to see the famous white helmet back out on the track. The relaxed and flowing style is as evident today as it was in the great old days.

The display we have at The Revival this year of eighty of Stirling's greatest cars is a tribute to him. I am delighted, as a friend and an admirer, to be able to make my small contribution to this record of the cars, and his extraordinary achievements at this landmark in the life of one of Britain's true sporting heroes. Happy Birthday Stirling.

Mar.

Charles March

Mercedes-Benz Driving Academy

Learn to drive earlier and become a better driver

Sir Stirling Moss first got behind the wheel as a child, and began his motor racing career at just eighteen years old. At the Mercedes-Benz Driving Academy you can start from an early age too... as soon as you are 1.5 metres tall.

Mercedes-Benz

MORGAN
MATCHLESS

The fact that, as a boy, Moss grew up with his Mother's Aero Morgan, may have influenced his choice of first car. Cash winnings from his successful equestrian activities were saved and used in the purchase of a 1936 Morgan sports 2-seater, with V twin matchless engine and registration CXD 826. With forward planning, Moss's early application for his driving license benefitted from the casual scrutiny of the Licensing Office, which issued a license by return, without noticing Moss's age. Thus, a couple of weeks before his sixteenth birthday, Moss was on the road, behind the wheel of his own car. The first of what would be many keen starts.

The Sports
2-Seater

With 10 h.p. Side Valve
Water-cooled Engine .. **£110**
With 10/40 h.p. O.H.V.
W.C. J.A.P. **£120**

AGW 343

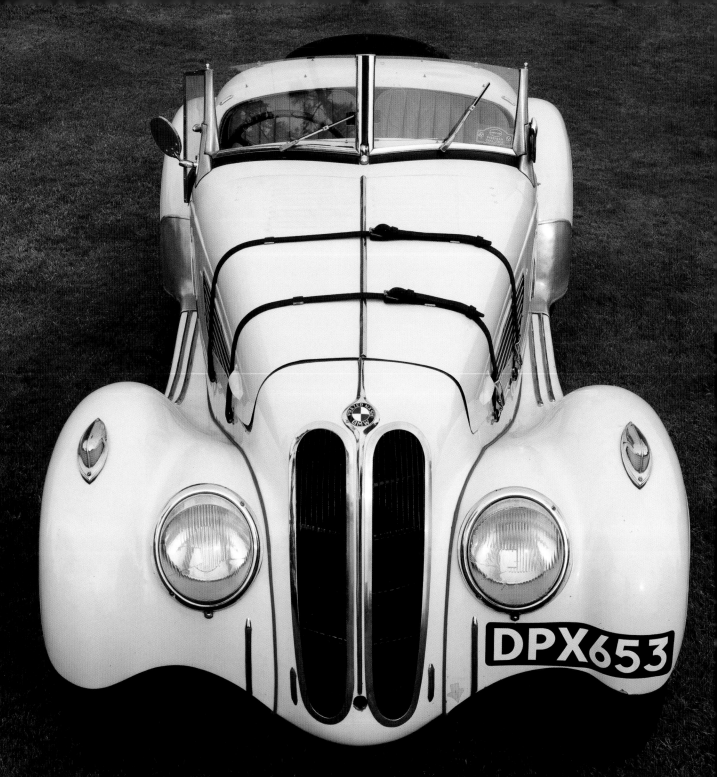

BMW 328

This 6 cylinder, 2 litre sports car produced a useful 80 bhp with handling to match and provided Moss with his first taste of competition. Winning the Cullen Cup at Harrow Car Club's 'Moss Trophy Trial', on 2nd March 1947, was an indication of things to come. Other trials and rallies in this car included a 1st class award at Eastbourne.

COOPER JAP MKII

The rise of a youthful and competitive Stirling Moss coincided with Cooper's production of a novel motor cycle engined racing car, in a fine example of great timing. Contributing cash winnings from his gymkhana events, Moss ordered a new MKII Cooper with 500cc Jap engine for his 18th birthday. The very first outing at Prescott on 9th May 1948 brought a 4th in class and press coverage. Next, a class win at Stanmer Park Hill Climb, Brighton, was followed by his first circuit race at Brough Aerodrome. First in heat and first in the race was further embellished with a first in the final handicap race. The motoring press took note, prophetically declaring Moss as 'one to watch in the future' while Moss continued with two more firsts and several FTDs for the rest of the year.

COOPER VINCENT MKIII

In 1949, Cooper cars produced a MKIII with lengthened chassis for those wishing to accommodate a 1000cc twin. Moss tested one with a Vincent-HRD engine installed, which was the most powerful unit available. He liked it and consequently ordered a new chassis. It then became apparent that Vincents would not sell Moss an engine, so a dry sump, 1000cc JAP engine was bought as an alternative. This proved to be a highly successful combination with two wins at Goodwood and a new class record at Prescott Hill Climb, as well as his first experience of continental motor racing

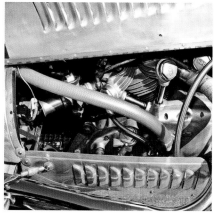

HWM

The HWM was a significant rung on the motoring ladder of Moss's career. Partners John Heath and George Abecassis of Hersham and Walton Motors had noticed the rising prominence of Moss in his 500 and 1000cc Coopers and invited him to drive for the works. For Moss, this was the first instance of being paid by a team to race. His debut as works driver was at Goodwood's Easter meeting 1950, where he achieved respectable 6th and 2nd placings.

OPC 2 is one of the four 1950 cars (3 works and 1 customer car), built as an offset single seater. In the Formula 2 race at Reims, Moss finished 3rd in OPC and a week later at Bari, 3rd again. This was quite an achievement, finishing behind the 158 Alfas of Farina and

Fangio but ahead of all the other F1 cars. HWM's (and later Moss's) chief mechanic, Alf Francis, said later that it was "the day Stirling Moss found himself". The following race at Naples ended in serious breakages, - Moss's leg, teeth and OPC - after the antics of a back marker took out the race leading Moss. The season continued at a hectic pace both abroad and at home with a notable win at Castle Combe after a titanic battle with Ken Wharton's ERA. OPC would be re-built and go on to have a second career in America with a Chevrolet engine, but that's another story.

COOPER MG

The first race at the 1950 Goodwood BARC June Members Meeting was a five lap scratch race and this one-off sports car, built by John Cooper the previous year, was entered. Running on trade plates to legally qualify as a sports car, it was powered by a newly installed MG 1250cc engine. Cooper had entered two races but for some reason he stood down for the first and invited Moss to drive. Motor Sport commented, 'Moss in the MG Cooper had trouble and was fifth', however, he took fastest lap at 74.5 mph in the process.

JAGUAR XK120

One of six aluminium bodied works cars, JWK 988 was owned by the accomplished journalist and driver, Tommy Wisdom. Conscious of the young Stirling Moss's talents behind the wheel, he offered Moss his car for the 1950 Ulster TT that was to be held on the new road circuit at Dundrod. Despite a less than spectacular practice and appalling weather during the race that saw tents blown away, Moss drove superbly to win. Peter Whitehead was second in HKV 500, another XK120 that Moss would race in the 1951 Mille Miglia. The publicity generated from Dundrod, for both car and driver, couldn't have been a sweeter introduction for Moss to the Jaguar marque. The following day was his 21st birthday.

COOPER JAP MKIV

In 1950, the FIA officially recognised 500cc racing as International Formula 3. After the 'two – way' MK III (500 or 1000cc) of the previous year, Moss concentrated on his 500cc MKIV. At Silverstone, 'swapping the lead ferociously with Aiken's Iota-Triumph' ended with a seized piston on the final corner and coasting over the line for second place. For Moss's first experience of the Monaco circuit, a new Sloper Jap was fitted to the Cooper and victory was achieved in both heat and race. A month later, Moss gave a masterful demonstration at Brands Hatch, winning five events including the 500cc championship. After another visit to Brands Hatch in August, the hunt was on to secure a Norton engine and develop the car further.

A WINNING TEAM

1951 INTERNATIONAL
GOODWOOD
MADGWICK CUP

1ST STIRLING MOSS (H.W.M)

2ND LANCE MACKLIN (H.W.M)

3RD GEO. ABECASSIS (H.W.M)

ALL ON **VIGZOL**
MOTOR OIL

HWM SENDS ITS BEST 80TH BIRTHDAY WISHES TO SIR STIRLING MOSS. WE WON TOGETHER IN 1951, THE SAME YEAR HWM BECAME AN AUTHORISED ASTON MARTIN DEALER, AND ARE BOTH STILL VERY MUCH IN BUSINESS TODAY!

HWM ALTA 1951

Following the successful 1950 season, HWM decided to build four new team cars with newly designed tubular chassis and proper single seater configuration, while retaining the 4 cylinder Alta engine. The first race outing was again the Easter meeting at Goodwood, with Moss winning the Lavant Cup and coming 5th in the Richmond Trophy. After this promising start, engine misfires, transmission problems and sheer bad luck intervened with annoying frequency throughout the season. In September it finally came good with Moss leading a 1, 2, 3 victory for the marque and setting a new lap record at Curragh in Ireland. Three weeks later Moss headed another 1, 2, 3 in the Madgwick Cup at Goodwood and set fastest lap, before concluding the season with a hard fought Formula 2 win at Winfield in Scotland, from teammate Abecassi's similar HWM.

JAGUAR XK120

Perhaps keen for brighter publicity after the un-spectacular 1950 Le Mans results, Leslie Johnson persuaded the works to prepare his car, JWK 651, for a high speed record attempt at Montlehery. The aim was to average 100 mph for 24 hours. Moss, sharing the driving, set off at 17.15 hours on 24th October 1950 for the first spell. 24 hours later the record was in the bag. Averaging 107.46 mph for the 24 hour period, the last hour covered 112 miles and the quickest lap was an impressive 126 mph.

ASTON MARTIN DB2

One of the three famous 1950 Le Mans team cars, VMF 65 gave Moss his introduction to the cars from Feltham. After a crash on the way to Le Mans, and finishing the TT 2nd in class, VMF was loaned to Moss and co-driver, Lance Macklin, for the 1950 Daily Express 1000 mile run. However, a penalty-free performance on the road section was let down by the results from the final driving tests. After a road test in 1951 for Autosport by John Bolster, VMF was put back in competition tune and sold to Rob Walker who, a few years on, would play a significant role in Moss's career.

VMF 65

KEIFT NORTON

A small team of skilled enthusiasts including Moss, invested much thought and design theory into the production of this prototype F3 car, that was underwritten by Cyril Keift. Built in 14 weeks, its first outing was at the 1951 Whit Monday Goodwood meeting, where its impressive win inspired many favourable column inches in the motoring press. Setting a new ½ litre lap record, receiving the 500 Trophy and a £200 prize, doubtless explained the comments of one motoring hack: "each time round, Stirling patted his car and grinned cheerfully to his pit!" Further wins followed at Silverstone, Zadvoort and Brands with more the following season at Castle Combe and Brands Hatch. At the 1952 Brussels GP, avoiding a major pile up resulted in somersaulting into straw bales with consequent alterations to chassis geometry. The car may have been written off but not the memory and the Keift remains one of Moss's all time favourites.

MORRIS MINOR

As with the Austin 7, so the Isigonis designed Minor proved a popular road, and sometimes competition, car for millions of people, including one Stirling Moss. Registered MMM 771, Moss's trusty Minor, served him well whether nipping down to Goodwood or venturing further afield, as when visiting Ferrari in Modena after the 1951 Exlen race in Switzerland. With the addition of some 'go faster' accessories at least one speeding ticket was received and the well known quip: "Who do you think you are, - Stirling Moss?", probably derived from one of these. In 1951, the Chiltern Night Trial was entered with a friend, but light-hearted fun got in the way of accurate map reading and hopes of success! Endorsed in the Sunday Times by Moss, he wrote: "I gave the Minor a severe test and I was delighted with its performance".

JAGUAR C TYPE 005

Stirling Moss first raced a C Type Jaguar in the 1951 Le Mans (ret.) and had achieved some important wins at Dundrod, Goodwood and Silverstone by the time he came to drive MDU 212. Offered the drive by private owner Tommy Wisdom, Moss persuaded Bill Heynes to fit the new 'disc' brakes for his entry in the 1952 Reims GP Sports Car Race. Despite serious fatigue caused by the cockpit heat, Moss won and provided the first major win for Dunlop disc brakes. Later entries brought firsts at Boreham, Turnberry and at Goodwood, in the September Sports Car Race, where despite setting a new lap record at 85.37, Moss finished second to Tony Rolt in XKC 011

FRAZER NASH LE MANS REP.

Designed for racing and as a road-going sports car, with a rugged chassis and engine supplied by Bristol (to FN spec.), the model attracted competitive enthusiasts from the start. In 1950, driving David Konay's VMC 701 at Castle Combe, Moss won from Crook's similar car. WMC 181 belonged to Sid Green and was loaned to Moss for both the 1951 and '52 British Empire Trophy at Douglas, Isle of Man. He won and set the fastest lap in '51 but was unable to repeat the performance the following year when an electrical fault forced retirement. The next month Moss took pole position at the Monaco Sports Car GP in XMG 6, but a problem with a rear wheel fixing spoilt the promising start and he retired while leading.

JAGUAR C TYPE 011

POV 114 was a works car that Stirling Moss first drove at the inaugural Goodwood nine-hour race in 1952. Sharing 011 with Peter Waiver they had a five-lap lead when an axle bracket failed. Time lost effecting repairs resulted in finishing fifth but they still won the over 3 litre class. The following year, the works fitted a full width screen for the Mille Miglia with Moss and Morris-Goodall to drive. Annoyingly, a twisted axle forced an early retirement. Fortunes improved in the British Empire Trophy on the Isle of Man with Moss finishing fourth in 011, following which, the pair carried out some special tyre evaluation work for the factory.

MOSS & LAWSON
TRIALS SPECIAL

Built by Stirling Moss's father in 1954, the Moss & Lawson Special exemplified
the Ford 10 engined Mudplugger, that was so popular in the fifties. Moss's
personal foray into the sport was at the wheel of the Harford III, which has
since disappeared in the mists of time. However, in the 1952 Kitching Trophy
Trial, he gained a Souvenir Award, beating team-mates Parnell and Bolster.

JAGUAR
XK120 COUPE

In August 1952, Leslie Johnson decided to attempt an improvement on the 1950 24 hour record at Linas-Montlehery, by averaging 100 mph for a whole week. LWK 707 was supplied by Bill Heynes for meticulous factory preparation. The same team of Moss, Fairman, Johnson and Hadley was chosen to share three-hour stints at the wheel. Four world records were smashed before a broken rear spring ended the official attempt according to FIA rules. The team, however, decided to repair and carry on anyway to achieve their goal. This they did averaging 100.31 mph for seven days and nights. A board was later displayed which read: 'For Sale, Jaguar Coupe, one owner, only 7 days old – small mileage'!

HAPPY BIRTHDAY, SIR STIRLING

From one veteran of the track to another. With best wishes from The Sunday Times.

1920
Motor Matters column by Gerald Biss appears in The Sunday Times.

1936
Humfrey Symons writes the first of his Motor Notes. The column runs until 1939.

1961
A Picture History of the Motor Car by Piet Olyslager, a Sunday Times Book Publication, is issued in 20 miniature volumes priced 2/6 each.

1968
Judith Jackson — the wife of British racing driver Peter Jopp — assigned to report on motoring. She becomes Motor Editor in 1977.

1968
The Sunday Times/RAC Motoring Atlas is published for the first and only time.

1976
First motoring column in the Scene section. It deals with the problems of wintry weather.

1993
Jeremy Clarkson writes his first motoring article for the paper, on the Aston Martin Vantage.

2002
Launch issue of Driving, our first separate motoring supplement.

2009
With its stand-alone supplement, InGear, The Sunday Times is considered the best quality newspaper for motoring.

APPOINTMENTS MAGAZINE NEWS REVIEW BUSINESS SPORT INGEAR HOME MONEY TRAVEL CULTURE STYLE

THE SUNDAY TIMES

For all you are.

JAGUAR XK120 COUPE

LVC 345 was purchased direct from William Lyons by Stirling Moss and sported a unique colour scheme of opalescent pale green over cream. Inviting Gregor Grant to join him, the pair entered the 1952 Lyons-Charbonnieres Rally, organised by the Automobile Club de Rhone. The marking system caused much controversy but they finished second in the over 3 litre class, helping to create a united first, second and third finish in class for Jaguar. A final competitive outing in the MCC Daily Express Rally again won first in class, despite problems with reverse gear selection.

BRM V16

Designed to produce an amazing 600 bhp
from a supercharged 1.5 litre engine, BRM
carried the Grand Prix hopes of a nation that
sadly proved unfounded. Following brief
tests in 1951 at Folkingham and Monza, both
plagued by mechanical problems, Moss was
asked by Raymond Mays to write a test report.
The only favourable comment concerned the
brakes, which were the first use of discs in a
Formula 1 car. Disappointingly, BRM withdrew
their entry for the 1952 Turin GP, finally
entering Moss in the Dundrod Ulster Trophy
that June. Somewhat predictably, a boiling
engine and cooked clutch forced retirement
and Moss never drove the V16 again.

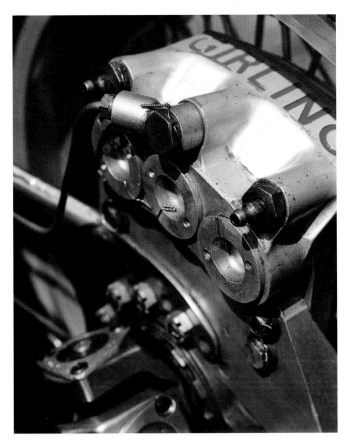

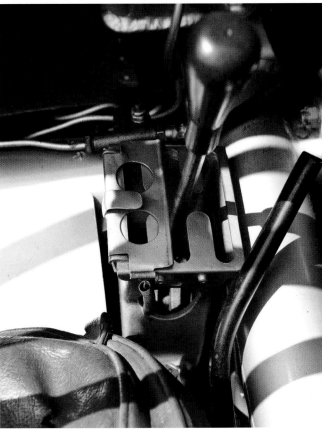

JAGUAR MKVII

LWK 343 was originally prepared by the works as a press entry for the 1952 Monte Carlo Rally, to be driven by Raymond Baxter and Gordon Wilkins. In May 1952, it was entered for circuit racing at Silverstone and in Stirling Moss's hands won the Production Touring Car Race. The victory was repeated convincingly in 1953 but not in 1954, when a jammed starter prevented a hatrick. Moss gave a fine performance finishing third behind the MkVIIs of Appleyard and Rolt, all three of them sharing fastest lap.

JIM STOKES WORKSHOPS Ltd.

CONGRATULATIONS, Stirling !!!

HAPPY 80TH

on all of your achievements
throughout your long and
successful career.

Happy Birthday from all at JSWL

CONNAUGHT A6

Connaught Cars Ltd., sent three cars to the 1952 Monza Grand Prix to be driven by Moss, Poole and the firm's financial backer, McAlpine. Moss, driving A6, was outpaced by the Ferraris, but rose to seventh place before the 'peculiar sounding engine' described in the press report, turned out to be a broken rocker – and he retired. In 1953, gear box failure prevented a start in the Ulster Trophy at Dundrod. A month later at Zandvoort, Moss made a magnificent start but a long pit stop to remedy a disconnected fuel lead hampered any high hopes and he finished ninth. He was, however, the first placed British car in the results.

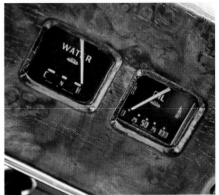

HUMBER SUPER SNIPE

The Rootes publicity department came up with the idea of driving from Oslo to Lisbon in 90 hours to demonstrate the model's reliability, speed and toughness. The route was to be via 15 countries, covering 3,280 miles with Moss and Leslie Johnson to share the driving of MRW 671. Leaving Oslo on December 2nd at 2am, severe winter weather lay ahead with blizzards and icy roads blighting them as far south as Italy. From Monaco to Lisbon, the temperature relented a little but still 1200 miles had to be covered in 24 hours... which they did, arriving in Portugal within the deadline by one minute! In a call to Rootes, Moss praised the performance and commented it had been "tougher than a Monte Carlo Rally".

HAPPY BIRTHDAY
AND BEST WISHES

SUNBEAM-TALBOT 90 MK2A

In 1952, together with Desmond Scannell and John Cooper (of Autocar), Moss entered his first Monte Carlo Rally in a Sunbeam-Talbot 90 and finished a very strong 2nd.

For 1953, the official Sunbeam-Talbot entry consisted of two teams of three cars, one of which, MWK 17, was driven by Moss and his 1952 crew. Mild weather, in contrast to the previous year's event, meant that over 200 crews attracted no penalties, thus putting a greater importance on horsepower in the regularity tests. Moss and crew finished 6th overall and their team succeeded in winning the prestigious Charles Faroux Team Trophy. It was the first time a British make of car had secured the Trophy for 21 years.

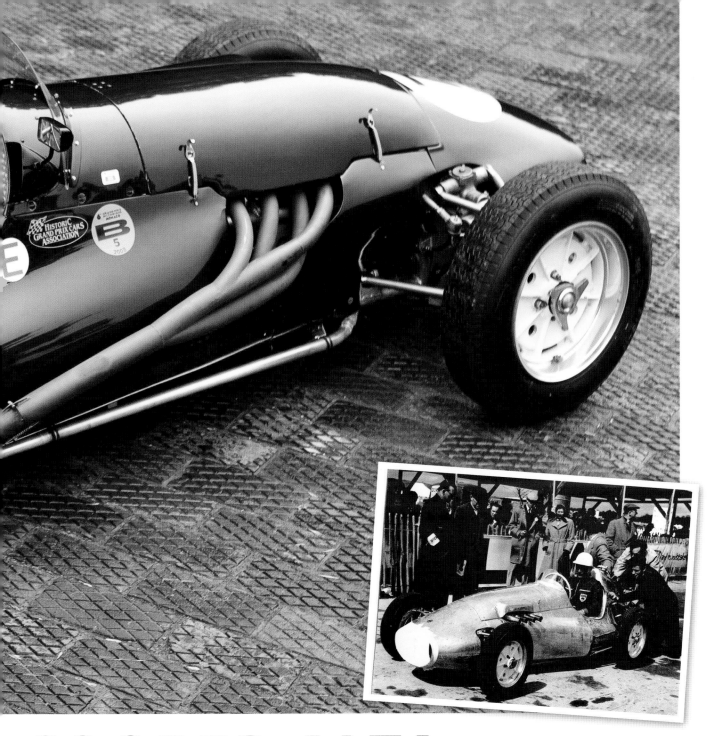

COOPER ALTA

This project was originally conceived by Ray Martin, Tony Robinson and Alf Francis as a modified Cooper chassis with a 4 cylinder Alta engine. Much last minute cutting and shutting went into assuring its debut in 1953 at the Goodwood Easter meeting. Autosport thought the disc brakes worthy of a photograph (first F2 car to use discs), but also noted 'Moss's Cooper Alta did not have the proper springs and had wedges inserted to enable it to run'. Together with chassis and brake problems, finishing 7th was a case of triumph over adversity. This was followed by Silverstone (9th), Crystal Palace (5th), Rouen (unc) and Nurburgring (6th) - before the French GP at Reims where the clutch burst, shattering the bell housing in the process and forcing a long walk back to the pits. For the German GP a month later, a standard chassis was ordered.

SUNBEAM-TALBOT ALPINE

Early in 1953, Moss and Sheila Van Dam recorded some high-speed times at Jabbeke and Montlehery to publicise the new convertible 'Alpine' model. Later in July, Moss was entered for the 16th Rallye International des Alpes in one of the six factory prepared cars, and nominated as driver for MKV 21. Finishing penalty free, as he had in 1952, Moss won a second Coupe des Alpes trophy and the chance of a hatrick in 1954. By common consent the 1954 Alpine rally was a tougher affair, which combined with atrocious weather, was to see only 37 finishers from 83 starters. MKV 21, again with Moss and co-driver John Cutts, finished 'clean' and in so doing, Moss won a coveted Coupe des Alpes d'Or (Alpine Gold Cup) for three consecutive un-penalised finishes – only the second driver to win such an award.

COOPER NORTON MKV

The extra power of the Norton dohc engine made it a popular, if hard to acquire power source for the Cooper chassis. Moss fitted his just prior to Silverstone, August 1950, and set a practice time that was actually faster than nine of the Formula 1 cars could achieve! Securing pole, fastest lap and outright win, was an excellent result to the race described as 'the most exciting of the day'. Further outings at Brands Hatch and Goodwood netted two second places before a spell of record breaking for Keift Cars. This would lead to future 500cc adventures in a different chassis.

TOJEIRO MG

In 1953, Lionel Leonard and Cliff Davis acquired two virtually identical cars with chassis built by John Tojeiro. Both cars had curvaceous aluminium bodywork, similar to the earlier Cooper-MG that had copied the styling of the Barchetta Ferrari 166. Davis' car (LOY 500) received a 2-litre Bristol engine and became the inspiration for the AC Ace, while Leonard's car (LOY 501) had a supercharged MG XPAG engine of just under 1.5 litres. It enjoyed a varied international career through 1953 and '54 and was known as both Tojeiro-MG and Leonard-MG. Moss was invited to drive it in the 1954 British Empire Trophy race at Oulton Park. In the first heat Moss finished third behind the Lotus-MG and Connaught of Peter Gammon and John Coombs respectively. In the final, however, on lap 12, while running second to Gammon's Lotus-MG, the crank broke at Lodge Corner and Moss retired letting Coombs into third place.

OSCA MT4

Moss had hoped for a Jaguar entry at the 1954 12-hour Sebring race, but it did not materialize and he accepted instead an invitation to drive for Briggs Cunningham, sharing a 1½ litre Osca with Bill Lloyd. In a 12-hour process of attrition, bigger and more powerful Lancias and Astons fell by the wayside until only Taruffi's Lancia was ahead of Moss. Finally, this too succumbed to engine maladies and Moss took the lead to win his first big international race since Reims in 1953. With three examples of the marque in the first eight finishers, and 1, 2, 3 on the performance index, Sebring 1954 was an Osca occasion. Maybe, fond memories have a bearing on the current Osca that Moss races today.

JAGUAR D TYPE

Building on the success of the C Type, the D Type benefitted from a new monocoque chassis clothed beneath even more aerodynamic bodywork. One of the very first works cars, XKC 403, was prepared for the 1954 Le Mans, with Moss and Pete Walker to drive. Just after midnight, brake failure caused a rapid exit down the Mulsanne escape road and retirement from the race. Earlier, Moss had been timed over the measured kilometre at an incredible 172.87 mph! A month later, at the Reims 12 hour race, the same pairing again retired, this time experiencing transmission problems. For the RAC TT at Dundrod, Moss drove a new works car, XKD 406 (3CPF) fitted with a 2½ litre engine to take advantage of the handicapping system. Running well till late in the race, the oil pressure faltered and Moss pushed the car over the finishing line to qualify for 18th place.

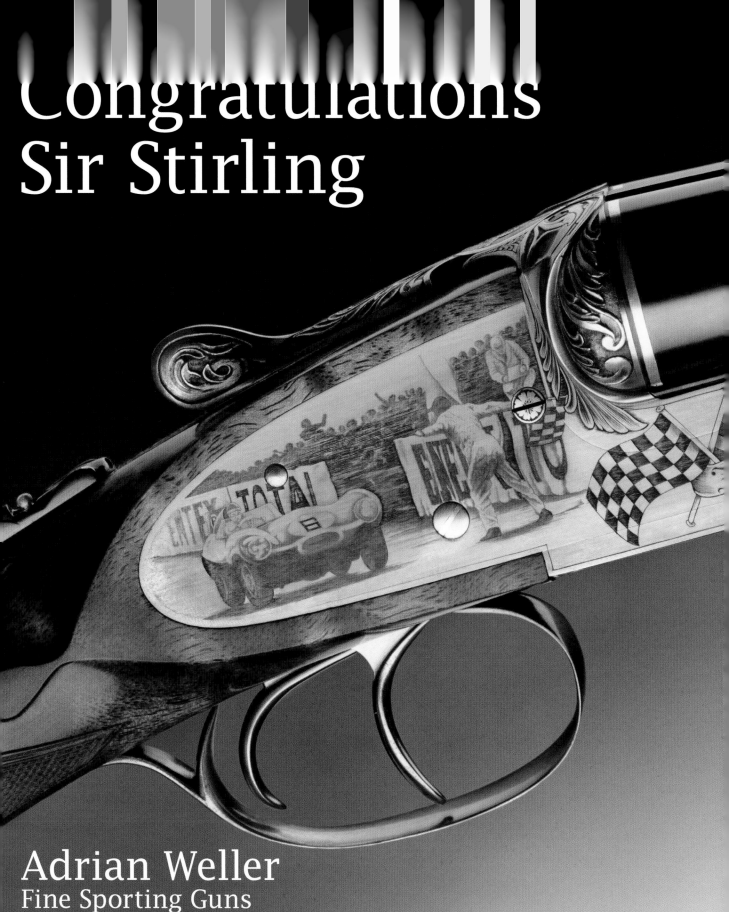

Congratulations Sir Stirling

Adrian Weller
Fine Sporting Guns

Tel +44(0)1403 713760 Fax +44(0)1403 711484 Mob 07977 403848
Email: aweller@finestsportingguns.com Web: www.finestsportingguns.com

LISTER BRISTOL

Originally registered MVE 303, BHL 4 was usually piloted by Archie Scott-Brown and regularly thwarted by Roy Salvadori's Maserati during the 1954 season. Keen to see if Moss's driving could improve matters, Scott-Brown offered him a drive at Goodwood at the September meeting. "Salvadori drove like one possessed with the Lister ever in his mirror", reported one journalist, "while Moss squeezed every ounce of power he could find". The last lap was a thriller with Moss alongside at Woodcote. The Maserati held on through the chicane and Moss finished second to Salvadori by 3/5 second, with fastest lap as a consolation.

CONNAUGHT ASLR

VPF 272 originally belonged to private sports car racer, Peter Bell. In 1954, he invited Moss to drive the car in the Coup du Salon at Montlehery, which was a 150 km event for unlimited sports cars. Running among much larger machinery, Moss beat Peron's Osca to win the 1500cc class. The following year, a last minute deal with Bell, saw Moss once again in VPF in return for Bell driving Moss's 250F Maserati at Aintree. The Daily Herald Trophy at Oulton Park attracted 30 starters and having not practiced, Moss started from the back row. In a demon start, Moss passed a dozen cars before the first corner. The incredible pace continued with Moss's 1½ litre car ahead of many larger Jaguars, Aston Martins and Ferraris. Winning the 1500cc class and placed 7th overall, Moss averaged 78.34mph to Reg Parnell's winning 81.16mph in a 3 litre Aston Martin.

MASERATI 250 F 2508

One of the all-time classic Grand Prix cars, the 2½ litre Formula 1 Maserati 250F was suggested by Alfred Neubauer as the vehicle for a keen and aspiring Moss to gain further experience. An order was placed, a not inconsiderable sum of money changed hands, and at Modena on 5th May 1954, Moss got to test drive his new car – 2508. Four days later, debuting 2508 at Bordeaux, the press reported, 'Moss drove a fast, steady race into fourth place with his newly acquired Maserati, the only one of the marque to survive the distance…'.

Two races later, and Moss took his first win in 2508 at the BARC Aintree 200. A month later at Spa, with 3rd place behind Fangio and Trintignant, he earned his first points

towards the World Championship. By now, the factory couldn't fail to notice Moss's commitment and results, and invited him to run as a member of the official Maserati team for the German GP. Overnight the faithful 2508 received a coat of red paint to cover Moss's British green livery (retaining a green noseband), but disappointingly, a fine start ended after a single lap with a run engine bearing. Winning the Gold Cup and Formula Libre event at Oulton Park in a substitute works car while the factory rebuilt 2508, proved fine consolation and setting a new lap record was the cherry on the cake. 2508 was returned in time for some European GPs that included quickest practice in the wet at Pescara and a leading drive at Monza that finished with mechanical

failure – all quietly noted by Mr Neubauer's all seeing eyes.

Goodwood and Aintree followed, both races resulting in clear victories and setting fastest lap, before the final race of the season at Barcelona. With a suspected holed piston, Moss retired on lap 18, but Neubauer had been sufficiently impressed with Moss's season in 2508 to offer him a place in the Mercedes team the following year.

2508 remained with Moss, to be raced in events not entered by Mercedes and competed six times in 1955 and a couple more in '56. Crystal Palace on 21st May 1956 was to be the last time Moss raced 2508 and beneath the Whit Monday sunshine, the faithful, now grey painted, Maserati finished first by 3/5 seconds after a terrific dice with Emery's Emeryson.

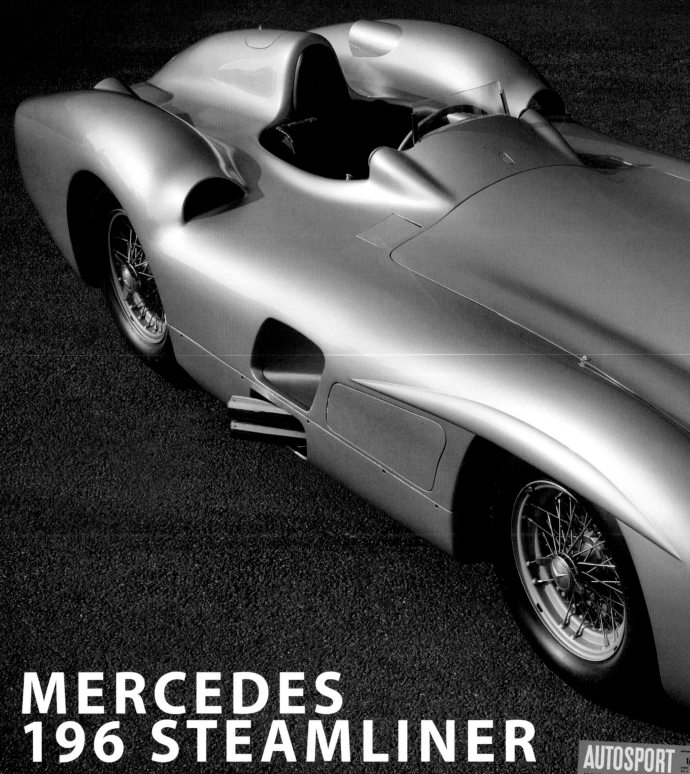

MERCEDES 196 STEAMLINER

The aerodynamic Mercedes Benz 196, known as The Streamliner, marked the factory's post-war return to Grand Prix racing and found immediate success with victory at the 1954 Reims GP. The open wheeled version was developed later in the year (as driven by Moss at Aintree) and the factory could choose body styles and chassis lengths to suit the venue. For the 1955 Italian GP at Monza, Moss was initially entered in a Streamliner with medium length chassis. Having practiced, it was decided a long chassis was more suitable and frantic activity at the factory produced two new chassis for the race, virtually overnight. In the race, a broken aero screen brought Moss into the pits after which some hard driving resulted in a new lap record. On lap 27, gearbox problems intervened, forcing retirement on Moss and a couple of laps later on his team mate, Karl Kling, as well.

MERCEDES
196 MONOPOSTO

Team manager, Alfred Neubauer, invited Moss to join the Mercedes-Benz team for the 1955 season. The venue for Moss's debut was the Argentine GP, where the intense heat took its toll and Moss's car expired with a vapour lock in the fuel system. Buenos Aires, Monaco, Spa and Zandvoort followed, all witnessing Moss driving so close to Fangio that the pair became known at the 'The Train'. None, however, was to be as close fought as the British GP at Aintree. Moss secured pole position by a margin of 1/5 second. Fangio led from the start until Moss passed him on lap three and by lap five the pair were beginning to lap the field. On lap 18, Fangio re-took the lead only for Moss to regain it on lap 26. "There was no faking about this business – both drivers doing all they knew to take and hold first place. . .", said Autosport. Taking the chequered flag for his first championship win, by just 1/5 second, was one of the most rewarding moments for Moss and the thousands of supporters who had just witnessed him become the first British driver to win the British Grand Prix. In honour of the victory, Autosport's traditional red-topped cover appeared, for that week, in white – Germany's racing colour.

AUTOSPORT

1/6

BRITISH GRAND PRIX

The British Grand Prix at Aintree
SOUVENIR NUMBER

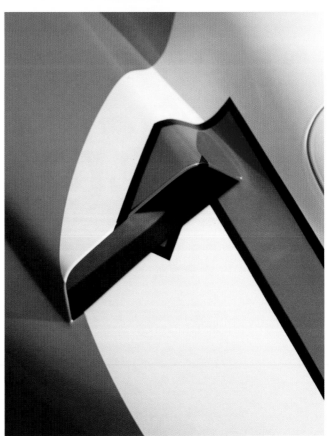

AUSTIN HEALEY 100S

The Healey 100S was a special version of the standard Healey 100/4, primarily designed to race and rally, as well as for favourable marketing. With a specially designed Weslake aluminum cylinder head, Dunlop disc brakes all round and an extremely light all aluminum body, some 55 examples were built following the 1954 prototype. On 13th March 1955, with an eye on some beneficial press coverage, Donald Healey invited Moss to drive a 100S with Lance Macklin at the Sebring 12 hour race. Despite racing against more powerful D Type Jaguars and 3 litre Ferrari's and Maseratis, their Healey finished a creditable 6th overall and 4th in the index of performance.

MERCEDES 300 SLR

Known as the 300 SLR for convenient press and publicity reasons, the original factory designation of 196 S was more indicative of its true origins. As a part of Mercedes Benz efficient determination to dominate Grand Prix and sports car racing, both types shared similar design principles with many parts interchangeable. Concentrating on the GP cars during 1954, it wasn't until the 1955 Mille Miglia that the 300 SLR made its racing debut. The story of Moss and Denis Jenkinson's legendary win is one of the most heroic and adrenalin fuelled in the history of motor racing. Meticulous preparation and testing, the famous 'Bog Roll' navigation notes, taking off at over 170 mph over blind brows and averaging nearly 100 mph for 10 hours over 1000 miles of ordinary Italian roads – are all a part of the epic tale that finished with Moss winning outright and setting a new course record.

After two 2nd places to Fangio in Sweden and Germany, and an ordered withdrawal from Le Mans while leading comfortably, (following the 'Levegh' disaster), Moss won the RAC TT at Dundrod in his Mille Miglia winning car, 0004. Despite a high-speed tyre burst that destroyed a chunk of the rear bodywork, Moss finished a lap ahead of Fangio. Post race a well earned birthday cake was shared out from the cockpit!

The final race of the season was the Targa Florio and the hard worked 0004 was entered for Moss and co-driver, Peter Collins. An off-road excursion nearly ended it all but back in the race 1st place was regained and Moss finished first, four minutes ahead of Fangio. In doing so, Moss secured the World Sports Car Championship for Mercedes Benz.

PORSCHE 550

Forever associated with James Dean, the 550 was Porsche's first official race car and powered by an air cooled, flat four 1500cc engine. Moss's first drive for the Stuttgart concern was at the 1955 Lisbon GP, where making up for a poor start, he was soon at the front and headed a triumphant Porsche procession, winning the Civil Governor's Cup race by 63 seconds from Mogveira in a similar car. Back in England, Moss arranged to share a car with Von Hanstein at the Goodwood 9-hour race, having the car prepared and delivered to the circuit by AFN Ltd. Taking over from Hanstein, the car lay 3rd in class but concentrated driving raised it to sixth overall and an easy class lead. Then, with less than an hour to go, a 'coming together' with the spinning Cooper Bristol of Tony Crook, took the damaged Porsche out – and with it a less than pleased Moss. Fortunes improved for the start of the 1956 season, with a double win at Ardmore, New Zealand. Winning the main GP in his 250F had a pleasing effect on his bank balance, which was further enriched when Moss won the Sports Car Handicap. Starting 3 laps behind meant over 90 cars had to be passed before he took the lead, and a local journalist wrote: 'Moss threaded his way through the field, never failing to acknowledge the slower drivers as they gave way to him, and blasting his horn on the corners to give the unwary due warning of his approach'.

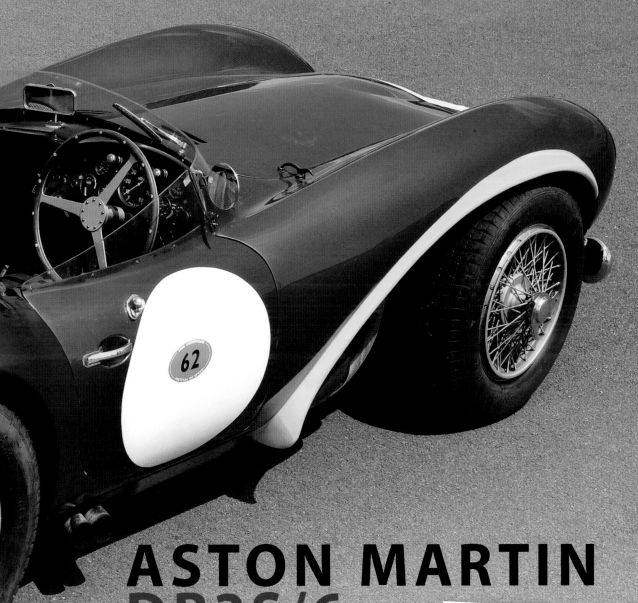

ASTON MARTIN
DB3S/6

Originally built as a fixed head coupe, '62 EMU was rebuilt by
the factory with open bodywork. After testing at Goodwood
in February 1956, Stirling Moss joined the Aston Martin team
and headed out to America for the 12 hour race at Sebring.
While running second between Hawthorn and Fangio, the
engine decided it had had enough which resulted in retirement.
Achieving second place at the Rouen GP brightened Moss's
fortunes which improved further at Goodwood's Easter meeting
in 1956, where he had a win and took fastest lap (in DB3S/5)

COOPER TYPE 39

Created with a full width enveloping sports body and central seating position, the T 39 began life as 1100cc and was increased to 1500cc for the MKII model. Driving works car RDG 474, Moss drove in the British Empire Trophy at Oulton Park and won the 1500cc class, returning a 1.57 lap against the 3 litre winning Maserati's new lap record of 1.56. Impressed, Moss ordered his own, which was registered 777 BPB, and was looked after by his mechanic, Alf Francis. The difficult handling characteristics at Aintree (5th) and Crystal Palace (2nd and 1st) were finally traced to an incorrectly jigged chassis alignment. A final outing at Rouen, shared with Phil Hill, ended with retirement and BPB was sold. Later in September at a very wet Oulton Park, Moss took a win in Willment's borrowed T 39 after his Aston DB3S victory earlier in the day.

Towergate Classic Motor congratulate Sir Stirling on 80 years of exceptional achievement

Sterling insurance cover
for your cherished classics

Tel: 0870 990 6060

www.towergateclassicmotor.co.uk

▲towergate classic motor

MASERATI 300S 3055

The Maserati 300S was first introduced in 1955 and quickly became a favourite of the cognoscenti. Briggs Cunningham bought the first three chassis, and 3051 (the first) made its racing debut on 1st May 1955 at Connecticut, and won with Bill Lloyd driving. Almost exactly a year later, on 27th May 1956, Moss and co-driver Behra, entered the Nurburgring 1000 kms in 3055. In practice, Moss was fourth behind three larger engined Ferraris, but the notorious 'Moss sprint' saw him first away under a promisingly cloudless blue sky. The lead steadily increased until over a minute was in hand before fate intervened and the rear suspension broke. The car was wheeled away 'hors de combat' but not the drivers who transferred to 3059...

Moss and the 300S won the Venezuelan GP in November, but just prior to the Bahamas Speed Week, where he was entered, the works sold the car. Sportingly, Bill Lloyd lent him the original 3501 – by now, well used – and Moss took another win nearly 1½ minutes ahead of Mansten Gregory's Ferrari.

MASERATI 300S 3059

The 300S had a robust tubular chassis, powered by a 3 litre engine, all beautifully covered by the purposeful lines of the Fantozzi designed bodywork. During the 1955 Le Mans 24 hour race, 3059 had been motoring strongly and holding second in class before a gear box problem forced withdrawal. The following year, it was entered as part of the works team, for the Nurburgring 1000 kms and driven by Taruffi and Schell. When the Moss/Behra car failed, team manager, Ugolini, hastily called in 3059 for them to take over. Having relinquished the lead to inherit 3rd place, behind the Ferraris of Fangio and De Portago,

first Behra and then Moss began to claw back the seconds. With seven laps to go, and a minute down, Moss was gaining nearly ten seconds a lap for a very close finish, when Fangio pitted for fuel. Into the lead went Moss, and increased the gap to take the chequered flag before an ecstatic crowd.

After winning the sports car race at Silverstone, at a speed nearly equaling the Grand Prix cars, Moss was entered for the Bari GP, again driving 3059, and led from start to finish.

In Moss's own words, "the 300S was one of the easiest, nicest, best balanced sports racing cars ever made".

"...if you really want to live, drive a 250F or a 300S at over nine-tenth's!"

Sir Stirling Moss

Happy 80th Birthday, Stirling

The above 1955 Maserati is just one example of the exemplary stock usually to be found in the showrooms of Fiskens in Kensington, London. For more information on the above Maserati 300S and details of other automobiles that we are currently selling, please do not hesitate to contact us using the details below.

FISKENS
FINE HISTORIC AUTOMOBILES

FISKENS, 14 QUEENS GATE PLACE MEWS, LONDON SW7 5BQ
Tel: +44 (0)20 7584 3503   Fax: +44 (0)20 7584 7403   Email: cars@fiskens.com
WWW.FISKENS.COM

ASTON MARTIN
DB3S/8

DB3S/8 was one of the 1955 team cars supplied new with disc brakes and a 12-plug head. As a signed driver for the 1956 season, Moss drove 743 HYX at the BRDC Daily Express meeting at Silverstone, in the sports car race for over 1500cc. Autosport reported: "As usual, first across the track and away was Moss, holding the DB3S in a power slide and covering the first yards on a diagonal"! The race began at a furious pace and a 'tangle' on lap 1 took out four potential winners. After the excitement the race settled down with Moss finishing in second place.

BERKLEY

An example of increasing promotional work and public interest in the Moss opinion, included testing the diminutively engined Berkley sports car in 1956 for BBC TV. With an automatic cine camera rigged up to the tail, and a microphone around his neck, Moss lapped the Goodwood Motor Circuit, adding his commentary for the benefit of BBC viewers. Notable points would have included the excellent acceleration from the tiny 322cc motor, effective braking, good road-holding and overall lightness of construction – the latter point illustrated, unconventionally, by four men lifting the car clear off the road - with Moss still seated inside!

MASERATI 450S

A newly designed, stronger chassis for the 450S, accommodated the immensely powerful new 4½ litre V8 engine. While in a class of its own as regards speed, it was frequently plagued by gremlins. Sharing 4501 with Fangio for the 1957 Argentine 1000 kms, Moss broke the lap record three times before the car itself broke, during Fangio's stint. For the Mille Miglia, the works entered chassis 4505 with Moss and Jenks to drive. Starting as favourites, and hoping to repeat their 1955 win, they set off, but barely 10 miles from the start the brake pedal sheared and their race was over. Repaired in time for the Nurburgring 1000 kms, Moss took the lead on lap 8 only for a rear hub to shear on the following lap. Finally, the sun shone on the 450S at the Swedish GP with Moss and Behra winning in 4503.

A final outing at Venezuela reverted to form. An amateur pulled out in front of a fast travelling Moss, wrecking both cars. The remaining 450S of Behra was taken over by Moss and then Shell; it too collided with a works 300S , in what was refered to as the 'Caracas chapter of accidents'.

VANWALL

The Vanwall was the car that would bring Moss his long yearned for wish to race, and win, a Grand Prix in a British car. The company's racing debut at Silverstone in May 1956, saw Moss in VW2 take pole, equal the lap record and win outright. Signing to drive for Vanwall in 1957, the season began with Syracuse and Goodwood blighted by small and frustrating snags. Fortunes changed however, for Aintree. Having led from the start, a faulty magneto prompted the decision to take over Tony Brooks' VW4 that was lying ninth. Determinedly working up through the pack and setting the first 90 mph lap in the process, Moss took the chequered flag in front of an ecstatic crowd. Thus, with Brooks' initial help, Moss became the first Britain to win the British Grand Prix in a British car. As Autosport put it: "everyone who was present went home realizing that history had been made." The season continued with wins at Pescara and Monza.

1958 proved to be rather black or white as regards results with either wins or retirements and one 2nd place at Reims. Moss changed the front wheels on VW10 for traditional wires, as at high speed, the airflow directed onto the back of the cast alloy wheels was affecting steering stability. Moss winning at Zandvoort, Oporto and Cassarlarco won the World Constructors' Championship for Vanwall's Mr Vandervell. The Drivers' Championship went to Mike Hawthorn by a single point, but some sporting testimony from Moss was a part of that story.

POET AND PEASANT (DB3S/9)

BY GODFREY SMITH IN THE SUNDAY TIMES OF SEPTEMBER 16TH, 1956

"I first began to regret the idea somewhere near Haslemere. It was a pleasant sunny afternoon, and I was bowling along between stately Surrey oaks in my Morris Minor at a steady forty miles an hour. The notion that I should shortly be travelling nearly a hundred miles an hour faster seemed incredible, and not a little dismaying.

"I had never travelled very fast in a car before. I had once driven a Renault Fregate flat out on the road to Le Mans, but even that amounted to only a wretched eighty-four miles an hour. Despite a mild interest in motor sport acquired through family enthusiasms, I was and am, a very average driver – in the colourful parlance of the racing fraternity, I am a peasant.

"Nevertheless, I was excited by the possibilities for a writer in the limit of any human experience. And one day over a lunch a few months ago Stirling Moss offered to take me out with him. It was Spring and the idea seemed, at that distance, highly agreeable.

"He commands an annual income a Prime Minister would be glad to own. His name is a household word. "Who do you think you are – Stirling Moss?" is part of the ordinary driver's vocabulary of abuse. He is a schoolboy's hero, one of the dream parts played by the Walter Mitty in every man. He is also a master craftsman, still striving for the last tantalizing degree of skill which will bring him as near perfection as man will ever get.

"He was to drive me as fast as he liked in an open DB3S works car. It had been built only this year and had raced four times. Driven by Moss and Collins, it had come second at Le Mans, and had won the three-litre category. Moss had driven it to victory at Oulton Park only a few weeks before.

It would do about 15 mph down the Lavant straight at Goodwood. If you felt inclined to buy one, it would cost you £3,901.

"Lloyds had sportingly bet me 2,000 to 1 that I would neither kill myself nor meet with a number of other unpleasant eventualities.

"The first thing Moss asked after we had

"WHO DO YOU THINK YOU ARE - STIRLING MOSS?"

shaken hands was: "Did you bring a helmet? No. We'll find you one. The visor will help your eyes, and in any case it's sensible."

"He decided to take the DB3S for a few trial laps. He leaped in, pressed the starter and roared off round Madgwick Corner.

"Goodwood deserted is a very different place from Goodwood en fete. The stands seemed empty and forlorn and there was no one as far as the eye could see. No one, that is, but the three men Aston Martins had sent with the car. Two were mechanics, and the third was Roy Parnell, the racing superintendent and nephew of the famous driver. I strolled over to them.

"Parnell is a quiet pipe-smoking Midlander. "Have you ever been fast before?" he enquired. I confessed that I had not. "Ah, well," he said philosophically, "I expect you'll get a bit of a shaking."

"We heard Moss busily negotiating Lavant Corner on the other side of the track, his gear changes like some angry hornet in flight. He came thundering down the Lavant straight and into Woodcote Corner. Coming out he grazed the earth at the side of the track, and a puff of dust rose into the air. The mechanics laughed appreciatively, "He's really trying today." They looked me over in a slightly cynical way. "Don't you wish you hadn't come?" one asked sympathetically.

"Moss came in after three laps. He was wearing blue overalls and a pair ▶

of moccasins. In ordinary clothes he always seems uneasy. Now he looked in his element. The mechanics told me to tuck the ends of my trousers into my socks as if I was going cycling. I noticed with a pang of embarrassment that my socks were now revealed up to the world as a violent buttercup yellow.

"I was wearing a pair of suede boots, a grey lounge suit, and to this already incongruous ensemble I lowered the helmet they had found for me. Because of the size of my head, I could fasten the strap only in the last hole. I looked like an adipose Martian. Moss looked me up and down and grinned broadly. "You brave devil," he said ironically.

"If you want to say anything," he said, "do this." He waved his hand palm downwards. "I'll try to hear." He started the engine and we were away.

"DON'T YOU WISH YOU HADN'T COME?"

"To be frank, my first conscious thought was that Moss had gone berserk. He hurled the car into Madgwick Corner at such speeds that I was sure we would turn over. There was an appalling shriek from the tyres, and the first black acrid stench of the rubber assailed me.

"On that first lap I saw almost nothing. I did not exactly close my eyes, but I will admit to squinting. I was dimly aware that Moss was using his arms in a kind of legerdemain. Even in that first corner, I had been appalled to see him suddenly steer the wrong way, that is, left into a right-handed corner. It was done so quickly that I might almost have imagined it. Later he told me that he probably used as much left lock as right to get round a corner at that speed.

"When you are driving normally, the road unfolds before you in a pleasing, continuous flow. Trees, posts and pillars mark your orderly progression.

"But now I was presented only with disrupted snatches of experience. It was as if, instead of seeing a film unwind, I was watching an expert shuffler zip through a pack of cards. The road seemed to leap at me on one side, then the other, in random pieces of brute sensation. The line that marked the edge wriggled by us like some frantic white serpent.

"It was during my first lap that we left the road altogether and ploughed through the grass. My weight had led Moss into a very slight and very rare miscalculation. He knew a long time before most people, that he had made a mistake and, as he afterwards explained, he decided to cut his losses. Instead of fighting the car round the bend, as the ordinary motorist would do, he turned the other way and elected to go up on the grass.

"The odd thing was that this did not frighten me in any special way. I was already in the grip of a vast and complex re-action.

"It was compounded of strangeness, awe, exhilaration and panic. At first, my brain was only telegraphing urgent animal messages from my outraged body. It was rather like that moment when the dentist's drill hits the nerve. The body simply cannot believe the affront, and rebels, seizing the mind captive and clamoring for relief.

"The moment soon passed. Round Lavant, which is nearly a hairpin, I lost all sense of space and direction. The world seemed to spin round us as if we were the centre of a pre-Copernican system geared up a million times too fast. And then we were into the Lavant straight.

"Moss threw the car down the track with what seemed to me maniacal recklessness. The wind had blown my coat almost off. It had risen up under my armpits and the sleeves were up to my elbows. I was hanging on, not as if my life depended on it, but because I had convinced myself that it literally did depend on it. We seemed to be hammering a wall of solid air.

"Just before the pits there is a chicane – a wall built out half-way across the track to form a man-made obstacle. Moss hurled the car round in what seemed to me roughly the right direction and then, to my horror, when the bricks and mortar were just about to go by on the left he seemed to steer suddenly straight into them.

"I hastily snatched my left hand off the cowling for fear of breaking my knuckles. There were certainly only inches to spare. Moss grinned. It was only when he did exactly the same thing in each successive lap that I began to appreciate the precision of his driving.

"By about the third lap I had relaxed slightly from the condition of apparent rigor mortis into which I had frozen. Moss lifted a thumb as if to ask if I was alright, and I half-heartedly lifted a thumb in reply. I tried desperately to analyse my emotions, to collect the material for that piece of writing I had spoken of so airily.

"Racing drivers are often criticized for being inarticulate. "It's just a drive" is all they will say after a hair-raising race. In fact, the experience is eventually indescribable. It is in a different bracket of experience – a separate octave of sensation. You can know it or not know it. The words to describe it fail you.

"We came into the pits after five laps. I asked Moss a number of questions and he answered them at length. To illustrate what he had done, he took me round the course in his Standard Ten and went through the whole thing again in slow motion.

"We cruised along at forty miles an hour. It was delicious; like breaking into a guilty walk after running for ten miles in a cross-country race.

"Parnell had written down our lap times. We had gone round the second lap in one minute thirty-eight and six-tenth seconds. Moss would have expected to do two seconds less without the encumbrance of my weight. The lap record for our sort of car stands in the name of Mike Hawthorn. He went four seconds quicker, but that was during a race and in a Ferrari.

"As we cruised past Woodcote Moss pointed to the verge where he had thrown up the dust going round by himself. "There ought to be a wall there," he said, "but as there isn't we go over a little. It's poetic licence."

"Poetic licence! – it seemed an odd phrase to use. And yet, I reflected in the harmony and grace of what they do there is something not far removed from poetry.

"Moss waved goodbye and drove off to Chichester. I dawdled towards home. Near Guildford there was a sudden roar, and the Aston Martin went by, driven by one of the mechanics.

"I watched its red lights winking into the distance. It seemed immeasurably remote from the modest progress of my Morris Minor. Yet I felt a tenuous sympathy for those vanishing lights. A poet and a peasant may have little in common, but if their lives have overlapped by only a few minutes, it is enough."

ASTON MARTIN DB3S/9

Having signed to drive for Aston Martin in sports car races during 1956, the last two outings were at the wheel of DB3S/9. Sharing chassis no. 9 with Peter Collins at a damp Le Mans, the Aston gave away a good 500cc to the rival Jaguars and Ferraris. Moss led from a demon start, but was soon overtaken by the more powerful D-Types, and for 24 hours the first 3 places swapped continually until ultimately resolved in favour of the Ecurie Ecosse Jaguar. However, for the latter part of the race, Moss had had to do without second gear and although finishing 2nd overall, they were first in the 3 litre class.

Back in England, on September 16th, the 'Poet' treated the 'Peasant' to some exciting laps of the Goodwood Circuit. One week later, at a rain-soaked Oulton Park, the works entered four cars including Moss in his Le Mans car 3S/9. The motoring press reported, 'At times the cars were hidden in showers of spray. How Moss drove at the speeds he did, in such conditions was amazing.' Both fastest in practice and setting fastest lap, Moss took the chequered flag at the head of a 1, 2, 3, 4 Aston Martin victory, in the Daily Telegraph sponsored International Trophy.

MG EX181

One of two record-breaking cars built by MG in 1957, EX181 was basically powered by a BMC B series engine (as fitted to the Austin A55 and MG Magnette) to which twin overhead camshafts and a supercharger were added. The aim was to raise the Class F, international speed record from Goldie Gardiner's pre-war 203 mph to 240 mph and Moss was invited to drive. The diminutive and aerodynamic machine was designed by Sidney Enerver with the engine behind the driver, who lay virtually on his back – somewhat different from the Vanwall that Moss was currently used to!

All ran smoothly under John Thornley's organization and on Friday 23rd August 1957, five new international records were set by Moss.

ASTON MARTIN
DBR1/1

Developed as a lighter replacement for the DB3S, 296 RW was the prototype that first
ran in 2½ litre form at Le Mans in 1956. In 1959, the factory was focussing on Le Mans,
but Moss persuaded David Brown to enter DBR1/1 (now in 3 litre form) for the 1000 km at
Nurburgring. Co-driver Fairman experienced a near disaster in a ditch, which cost the pair
the lead but inspired one of Moss's legendary comeback drives. Moss retook the lead from
the Ferraris of Hill and Behra and won by 41 seconds. It was Moss's second consecutive win
at the 1000 km Nurburgring and as well as setting the fastest lap, it placed the Aston Martin
in a very favourable position to take the World Sports Car Championship.

296 RW

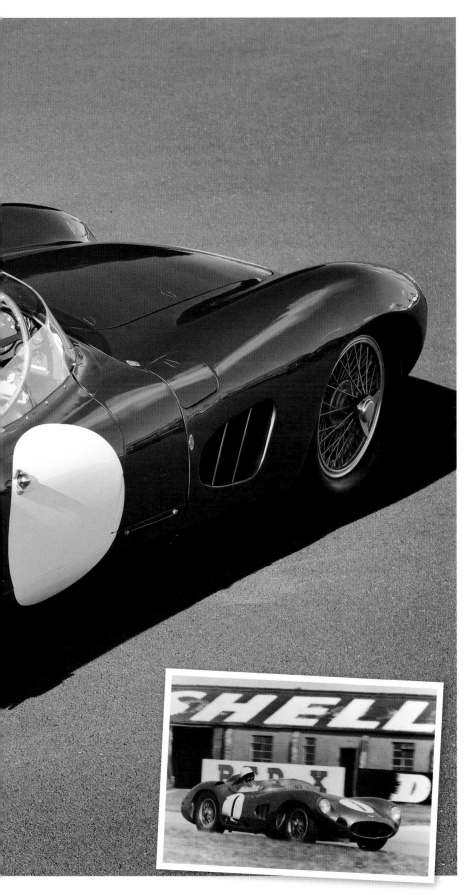

FERRARI 290 MM

Originally, Moss had been entered to drive Aston Martin DBR2/2 in the Nassau Trophy at the Bahamas Speed Week. However, in the preceding Ladies Race, Ruth Levin came unstuck in the DBR 2/2, rolling the car twice and leaving Moss without a drive. Some pit lane negotiations provided an alternative mount in the shape of a two-year old 3½ litre V12 Mille Miglia Ferrari, and entered by Temple Bull, Moss had his first drive in a Ferrari sports car. Third off the line, his initial battle was with Mansten Gregory and then Carrol Shelby (both in Maseratis) before permanently securing the lead on lap 34. As Moss crossed the line, nearly 2 seconds ahead of Shelby, he also became the first person to win the Nassau Trophy twice. As Autosport put it, "palm trees, calypso music, pretty girls in chic clothing, car talk, the sound of the surf splashing in the distance and expert dancing by the best racing drivers, all blended to made a memorable occasion"!

COOPER T43

A lengthened chassis was designed to comply with new championship regulations, and made available to paying customers. Designated T43, Rob Walker acquired one of the first and took it to the Argentine GP for Moss to drive in place of his unready Vanwall. With the competition comprising full- blown Formula 1 2½ litre machines, the little 2 litre Cooper was perceived as a 'David amongst the Goliaths'. Despite an eye injury, Moss qualified 7th in practice behind three Ferraris and three Maseratis. While Fangio led a Maserati/Ferrari battle, Moss in the T43 was consistently rapid and worked his way up the field until he was pushing Fangio. When Fangio pitted for tyres, Moss took the lead and for the final 20 laps maintained the finest of balancing acts between conserving his tyres and maintaining his speed. The Ferraris of Hawthorn and Musso chipped away at his lead, but with bald canvas streaked tyres, Moss crossed the finishing line to win by 2.7 seconds, and in so doing, gave Coopers their first F1 victory.

Coventry Climax

COOPER

ASTON MARTIN DBR1/2

In March 1958, Stirling Moss signed up with Aston Martin for sports car racing and made his team debut at Sebring in XSK 497. Setting a new lap record was some consolation for a broken gearbox that forced retirement and cost a victory. Happily, no such gremlins appeared at the Goodwood RAC TT race that year, where Moss headed an Aston Martin team (with co-driver Brooks), achieving first, second and third and setting a new lap record. For 1959, the works Sports Car Championship rested on the outcome of the Goodwood TT. Moss led in DBR1/3, which then caught fire while refuelling. Hastily taking over DBR1/2, which lay second behind the leading Porsche, Moss regained the lead to win, and in so doing, secured the Championship in Aston Martin's favour.

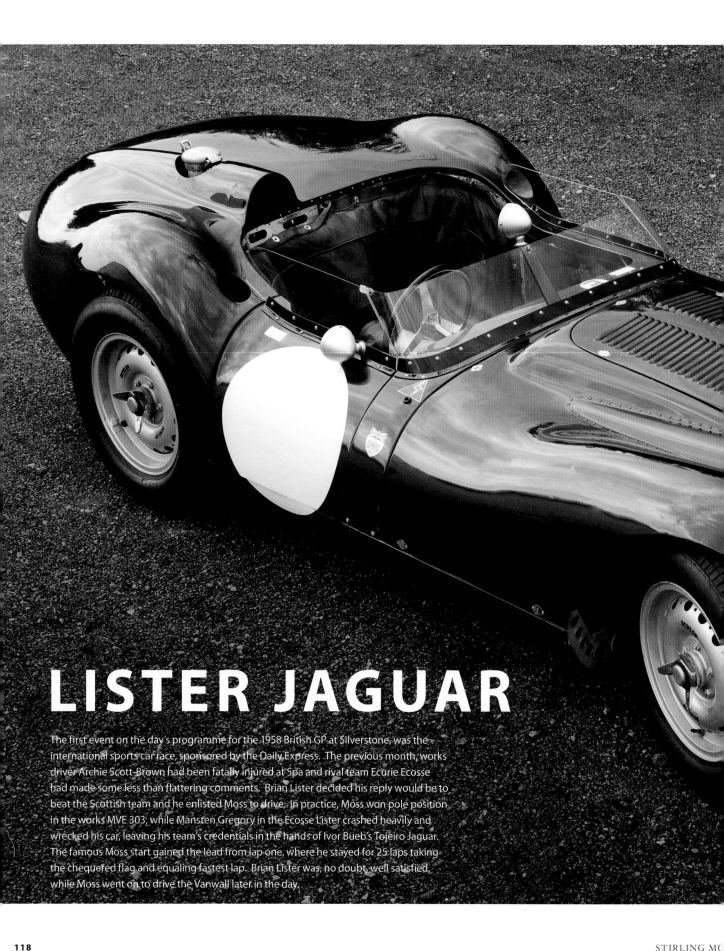

LISTER JAGUAR

The first event on the day's programme for the 1958 British GP at Silverstone, was the international sports car race, sponsored by the Daily Express. The previous month, works driver Archie Scott-Brown had been fatally injured at Spa and rival team Ecurie Ecosse had made some less than flattering comments. Brian Lister decided his reply would be to beat the Scottish team and he enlisted Moss to drive. In practice, Moss won pole position in the works MVE 303, while Mansten Gregory in the Ecosse Lister crashed heavily and wrecked his car, leaving his team's credentials in the hands of Ivor Bueb's Tojeiro Jaguar. The famous Moss start gained the lead from lap one, where he stayed for 25 laps taking the chequered flag and equaling fastest lap. Brian Lister was, no doubt, well satisfied, while Moss went on to drive the Vanwall later in the day.

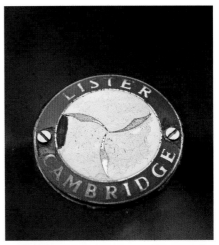

ASTON MARTIN DBR3/1 (1/4)

''NSK 693' was originally built by the factory as a one-off DBR3, essentially a DBR1 with newly designed front suspension and a short stroke engine. Entered for the 1958 sports car race at Silverstone, Moss took a class record for the first 3 litre sports car to exceed 100 mph lap speed. Unfortunately, on lap 14 the bearings cried 'enough' and the engine seized with inevitable retirement. The anticipated 300 bhp at 7000 rpm did not materialise and DBR3/1 was converted to standard DBR1 spec, in which guise it went on to have a distinguished career.

COOPER T51

As in '58, the 1959 international motor racing season opened with the BARC Easter Monday meeting at Goodwood. Rob Walker's Cooper F2/7/57, wearing the new 2½ litre Climax engine, was entered for the Glover Trophy with Moss to drive. Harry Schell's BRM led initially, appearing faster on the straights, but the Cooper showed better handling on the corners and on lap 10 Moss took the lead at St Mary's, keeping it to the end and also setting fastest lap. The standard Cooper gearbox was struggling with the increased power from the new engine and a fresh design was commissioned from Colotti and fitted for Monaco. The opening stages witnessed a great battle with Behra's Ferrari and Brabham's Cooper, "sometimes almost abreast or in line ahead as if tied by string". On lap 22, Moss took the lead and began to pull away, establishing a comfortable lead, only to retire on lap 81 with gearbox failure. '"He drove a masterly race showing virtuosity of the highest order", Autosport opined. Three weeks later, another gearbox problem would strike, while leading the Dutch GP at Zandvoort. The frustration of retirement was perhaps mildly alleviated in setting a new lap record at 96.6mph.

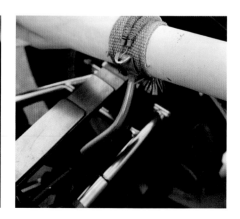

There are those who drive.
And those who are driven.

TRUSTED FOR CENTURIES
140 YEARS
· 1868 – 2008 ·

F&C Investments would like to wish Sir Stirling many happy returns on his 80th birthday.

F&C
Investments

ASTON MARTIN DBR2/1

Having previously driven at Nassau in 1957, Moss was again entered by the works in DBR2/1 for the first British race of the '58 season, at the Goodwood Easter Monday meeting. Making his customary speedy start, Moss led but Archie Scott Brown's powerful (and lighter) Lister Jaguar went past down the Lavant straight. A terrific dice ensued, with Moss setting a new lap record and regaining the lead, after which Scott Brown retired with steering problems and Moss continued to victory. The following week, DBR2/1 was again put to work at Oulton Park with Moss driving in the British Empire Trophy race. Having won the preliminary heat, the final began at a furious pace with Moss first, ahead of Cliff Alison's Lotus and Tony Brooks' Aston. Diminishing oil pressure did for the Lotus and Moss headed an Aston Martin 1 – 2 victory with Tony Brooks 2nd – both in DBR2s. The motoring journalists were impressed, one reporting that, 'Astons once again demonstrated what remarkably sound, fast cars and drivers they have – for there was no fuss or bother from either'.

COOPER T51

In August 1959, Rob Walker bought a new Cooper from the works and entered it in the German GP at Avus. With Moss driving, F2/19/59 had an inauspicious debut with an attack of gearbox maladies and consequent retirement. Three weeks later, at the Portuguese GP it all came right, starting on pole, setting fastest lap and finishing 1st. The only driver to complete the full 62 laps, one journalist wrote, 'on and on went the amazing Mr Moss, giving a display of driving skill that was an education in itself.' Next, at Monza, a strategic win over Ferrari came from consistently saving rubber and deciding to go through non stop, while Phil Hill's Ferrari pitted for rear tyres. The 150 mile Oulton Park Gold Cup witnessed a royal battle between the Coopers of Moss and Brabham, thrilling the large crowd. With seldom more than five seconds between them for the entire

race, Moss took the flag, together with a good chunk of the £3,650 total prize money, and set a new circuit record. The '59 world Championship rested on the outcome of Sebring and was between Moss, Brabham and Brooks. A new rear suspension modification worked well and Moss's practice lap times were five seconds quicker than anyone else. 'He made racing look so ridiculously easy' wrote Autosport. However, only six laps in, transmission trouble spelt the end of his race together with his championship dreams. The Glover Trophy at Goodwood in April 1960 was the final outing for Moss in F2/19/59. Driving at the top of his form and setting a new lap record of 102.13 mph was not enough to pass the new Lotus 18 of Innes Ireland. After 42 laps, and covering 100 miles, Moss finished second by just 2.8 seconds.

BRM P25

Having kept abreast of the P25 and its development since 1955, Moss tested a new works car at Goodwood in April 1959, and recorded the first ever 100 mph lap there. The first race entered was at Silverstone and a promising practice that bettered the lap record by 1½ seconds, ended with retirement in the race following brake failure.

The next outing in a P25 for Moss was at Reims, with chassis 2510, but a new lap record of 2 minutes 22.8 seconds was the sole consolation after a broken clutch and spin ended his race. A fortnight later at Aintree, again with 2510, Jack Brabham led from start to finish in his Cooper Climax but the fight for 2nd place between Moss and Bruce McLaren had the crowd on the edge of their seats. The closing laps struggle saw them share a new lap record with the outcome decided in favour of Moss by 1/5 second.

COOPER
T53

The new lowline Cooper was conceived in answer to the Lotus 18 and was designed to take either the 1500cc Climax for new F1 regulations, or up to 2.7 litres for inter-continental and Tasman events. In March 1961, Rob Walker bought chassis F1/7/61 with a 2.5 litre Climax engine for Moss to drive. The highlight of the Easter Monday meeting at Goodwood was a "stupendous duel" between Moss and Bruce Maclaren for the Lavant Cup, resolved in the former's favour by just 0.6 seconds. Appalling weather struck May Silverstone and illustrated Moss's genius as a wet weather driver, when he lapped the entire field to finish first. Back at Silverstone a couple of months later for the British Empire Trophy, the weather was kinder but the result was the same, with Moss setting fastest lap and lapping all except John Surtees and Graham Hill. A larger 2.7 litre Climax engine was fitted for 1962 and some antipodean racing. Two races in New Zealand finished with 2nd places while in Australia, at Warwick Farm, "Brabham, Moss and Maclaren were all pedalling on the limit", for Moss to be the eventual winner.

LISTER
JAGUAR COSTIN

The American privateer, Briggs Cunningham, purchased the first two Knobbly Lister Jaguars for his team in 1957 and he was keen to add the new Costin bodied Lister to his stable. In 1959, aeronautical engineer, Frank Costin, revised the bodywork in a not wholly successful attempt to improve the aerodynamics. 11 cars were built in total, of which two had Jaguar engines and one of these, registered BHL 123, was bought by Cunningham. After some testing by Moss at Silverstone, BHL was entered for Sebring, (together with one of the team's existing Knobblys), and in both practice sessions Moss was easily fastest. Co-driver, Ivor Bueb, did the first stint, followed by Moss who rapidly took the car from 3rd to 1st, passing the leading Ferrari of both Gurney and Behra. 'The faces in the prancing horse pits grew longer and longer', reported Gregor Grant for Autosport. A similar affliction awaited the Cunningham team, when the engine died having run out of fuel after miscalculations at a hasty pit stop. In getting a lift back to the pits on a motorcycle, Moss found himself disqualified for not walking. Taking over the team's Knobbly for the final laps prevented some thumb twiddling, but it was well down the race order with no serious hope of a position.

ASTON MARTIN DB4GT DP199

ANO 351A (design project 199/1) is the prototype DB4GT, which made its racing debut at Silverstone in May 1959, with Stirling Moss at the wheel. Driving for the factory, Moss qualified on pole, took first place and set fastest lap in a very satisfying performance. Two other outings in similar cars at Nassau in 1959 and Goodwood in 1960 also resulted in Moss victories.

MASERATI TIPO 60

The Tipo 60 was a newly designed sports car from the Maserati brothers, constructed from a collection of small diameter tubes, welded together to form a rigid space-frame. Initially referred to as the 'Spider's Web' and 'Spaghetti' Maserati, it became more commonly known as the Birdcage and was powered by a 2 litre, four cylinder engine. In May 1959, Moss tested 2541 at the Modena Autodrome, finding its lightness and excellent Dunlop disc brakes much to his liking. The first official outing of the year for Maserati, and first event for the new car, arrived on July 12th at Rouen, for the Coupe Delamare Deboutteville. Despite the efforts of Stacy and Ireland in Lotus 15s, Moss led comfortably from start to finish, lowering the lap record on several occasions and finally leaving it at 2 minutes 29.0 seconds.

RENAULT
DAUPHINE

To celebrate the 50th Anniversary of Bleriot's 1909 cross channel flight, the Daily Mail sponsored a race from Marble Arch to the Arc de Triomphe. Choice of transport was down to the individual, as was the departure date over a 10 day period and the winner was simply the quickest. At 8am on the morning of 13th July 1959, Moss set off from the London control in a Renault Dauphine, 'hotted- up' to Gordini spec. Including the hop over the Channel, courtesy of a Silver City, Bristol Freighter, Moss clocked in at the Arc de Triomphe an impressive 2 hours 47 minutes and 7 seconds later.

Captain Walker on a motorcycle and Lieutenant Commander Boaks on roller skates, left at the same time as Moss but took a little longer. The winner though, was Squadron Leader Maugham, who put his Hawker Hunter to good use and recorded the winning time of 40 minutes, 44 seconds.

Maybe not a level playing field, but the race was deemed great fun by all participants and a fitting tribute to Bleriot's achievement.

COOPER MONACO

The Type 49 Monaco was announced in 1959 as a replacement for the bobtail and was received with enthusiasm. Now with a conventional two-seater layout, it was designed to have both 1½ and 2 litre FPF engines and was immediately successful. Moss acquired his own car and got his friend Mike Keele, (of whose kart building business Moss was a director) to prepare and enter it. Aintree was their first outing and the pale green bodywork took a hard thump to the rear when Moss stalled on the starting line and the Lotus of Edward Greenall rammed him. The jolt did however get Moss started and he streaked off to make his way up through the field. Having worked up to 8th place, fate had other ideas when a burst oil pipe caught fire and Moss retired.

A trip to Scandinavia brought a win and the lap record at Karlskoga; then having won four of the six heats, another 1st on aggregate at Roskilde.

ASTON MARTIN DB4GT

Having previously driven the prototype DB4GT in 1959, and won at Silverstone, Moss enjoyed further success with the model, racing a loaned car at Nassau. For the 1960 Easter meeting at Goodwood, Moss was entered to drive the DB4GT, 0124/R for Tom Sopwith's Equipe Endeavour. Road registered 587 GJB and with a special lightweight chassis, Moss dominated the closed car category's Fordwater Trophy, starting from pole, setting fastest lap and taking the chequered flag.

MASERATI TIPO 61

The 1960 Birdcage Maserati had its engine size increased to 2.8 litres and was identified as Tipo 61. Driving for 'Lucky' Casner's team 'Camoradi', Moss put the increased engine size of 2461 to good use at the Cuban GP, by finishing first and setting a new lap record. A month later, at the Sebring 12-hour race, and again driving for Camoradi, a rear axle problem proved terminal and Moss, co-driving with Dan Gurney, was out. Both drivers and 2461 entered the 1960 1000 km race at Nurburgring, which took place during very unkind weather conditions. For once, the sprinting Moss was second man away, but before the completion of lap one, he was in the lead. While co-driver, Gurney, took his turn, a Ferrari caught fire while refueling and Moss rolled the blazing driver, Scarlotti, on the ground to extinguish his flames! Back on the increasingly foggy circuit, having regained time lost from the burst oil pipe, Moss took the chequered flag to win his third consecutive 1000 kms.

AUSTIN HEALEY
SEBRING SPRITE

Following the 1, 2, 3 success of the Austin Healey Sprites in 1959 at Sebring, Donald Healey, with works BMC backing, prepared two cars for the 1960 4-hour race. Driving 708 OAC, Moss was first away and though winning his class, finished second overall to Paul Richard's Abarth. For 1961, John Sprinzel had commissioned Williams and Pritchard Ltd., to build six special lightweight aerodynamic cars and one of these, Sprinzel's own car, PMO 200 was prepared for Moss. Despite a clutch that was struggling with the increased engine power and a significant speed superiority on the straights of the Abarths, Moss made up time on the corners and finished 5th overall. Intriguingly, PMO 200 is the only car to have been raced competitively by both Stirling and his sister, Pat, who raced it at Brands Hatch in 1960.

JAGUAR MKII

The reputation of the 3.8 litre Jaguar MKII, forever cast as the getaway car in Ealing Studio movies, was not without foundation as it was indeed a quick car. Offered a drive at the BRDC Silverstone International Trophy meeting in Tom Sopwith's example, registered JAG 400, Moss started from pole position. The front row consisted of four 3.8s in total and the press commented on "their enormous speed" plus the fact that just two seconds separated all four. For once Moss was second man away, but took the lead on lap 2 only to loose it amongst back markers. Finishing 2nd behind Salvadori's similar car, all four 3.8s had lapped the entire field.

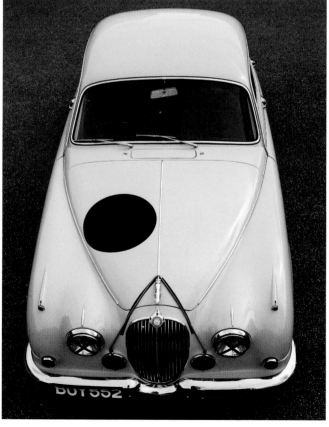

ASTON MARTIN
DB4 ZAGATO

22 XKX was the first DB4GT chassis to be bodied by Zagato, gracing their stand at the 1960 Earl's Court Motor Show. With some influence from the John Coombs dealership, Dick Wilkins financed the purchase for his friend Rob Walker, who painted it in his team colours of midnight blue with a white bonnet band. Walker then entered the 1961 Easter Monday Goodwood meeting with Stirling Moss to drive. Despite qualifying on pole for the Fordwater Trophy, Moss finished third behind the better handling Ferrari 250 GT SWB.

LOTUS 18

Sharing the same 2½ litre Climax FPF engine, the new Lotus 18 was a serious rival to the Cooper T51 and quickly became sought after. Privateer, Rob Walker, was one of the first owners and with Moss driving and winning at Monaco in 1960, gave Lotus their first F1 victory. The season continued with a notably bad crash at Spa and concluded in a replacement 18, with wins at Oulton Park and Watkins Glen. For 1961, Moss continued with the 2½ litre Lotus in New Zealand (retired) and Australia (1st) before returning to Europe and the new 1½ litre Formula.

Team Lotus kept the new 21 for themselves, so on May 14th 1961, Moss found himself sitting on the grid at Monaco in an outdated chassis and in the company of the more powerful Ferraris. Ginther's Ferrari led off the line, but on lap 14 Moss squeezed past. The pressure never relaxed but still Moss stayed ahead and in the drive of his life continued to do so, winning by a mere 3.7 seconds after 100 laps. Not seriously believing there was a chance against such formidable opposition, the 120,000 track spectators and millions of television viewers were treated to a magical, edge of the seat, race. 'It was Stirling Moss night in Monte Carlo…', reported the press, continuing unsurprisingly, '…the celebrations going on till daylight.'

RACING CAR SHOW

Racing Car Show Issue
MOTOR RACING
January 1961   Monthly 2/6

FERRARI 250 SWB 2119

The Ferrari 250 of the late 1950s received continual development and refinement, to the point in 1959, when the 250 GT SWB made its debut appearance at the Paris Auto Show. 2119 was ordered by Dick Wilkins, who engaged Rob Walker to prepare and enter the car for Moss to drive. Painted in the traditional Walker colours, its first outing was in August 1960, at Goodwood, for the RAC Tourist Trophy. After some close battling with Salvadori's Aston DB4 GT, it was quick pit work and tyre-changes that proved to be the deciding factor. Moss took the chequered flag securing his third consecutive TT win, and increased the lap record. At Brands Hatch, the quality of preparation was commented on, and fastest in practice paved the way for another win and new lap record – the press noting, 'Moss's Ferrari simply glided round making it look oh, so easy'!

To finish the year, a European winter was exchanged for the warmth of the Bahamas and 2119 entered in the Nassau TT. True to form, Moss and 2119 set fastest lap and won the race.

KEELE GO-KART

The popularity of kart racing spread from America to England with the first official race to RAC rules, held at Lakenheath in 1959. At this time, and following an introduction from talented engineer Mike Keele, Moss's full time race mechanic was Dick Tarrant. At the last minute, Keele decided to enter Lakenheath. Together with Tarrant's assistance and plenty of midnight oil, two karts were ready for the event and Keele-Karts was born. As a member of the "3Ks" (Three Kounties Karting Klub), Moss entered various events that did not coincide with his grand prix or sports car commitments, including Long Maston and the 1960 World Karting Championships in Nassau. Driving Aerial or Boltaco powered Keele-Karts, Moss became a director of the company, carried out promotional work and enjoyed a new form of motor sport.

LOTUS 18/21

As the 1961 season progressed, privateers were able to update their Lotus 18s with newer parts from the works, including rear suspension modifications and lighter, sleeker body panels from the 21. After six outings in the hybrid 18/21, which included wins at Brands Hatch and Nurburgring, Moss set off for the Swedish and Danish GPs, to drive a UDT-Laystall backed car, run by his father. Arriving late from the previous day's Goodwood TT Race, Moss missed practice and was therefore obliged to start from the back of the grid. In three laps, the pale green UDT chassis 916 was at the front, where it stayed to win, sharing fastest lap with John Surtees. A week later, the same combination of car and driver raced at Roskilde – a narrow and twisting circuit built in a disused gravel pit. The event was run in three heats, the aggregate of the three deciding the final positions; somewhat conclusively, Moss won all three.

Two further races in Rob Walker's 18/21 were at Modena (1st) and Watkins Glen, where failing oil pressure forced retirement while leading.

FERRARI 250 SWB 2735

For 1961, Dick Wilkins ordered a new special Competizione model to replace 2119GT and in June of that year 2375 was delivered, direct to Le Mans for Moss. The same business arrangements applied as for 2119, with the addition of Graham Hill as co-driver for the Le Mans 24-hour race. Running strongly, and even challenging the sports/racing cars, it all ended abruptly when a fan blade detached and severed a radiator hose, with dire consequences. At both Silverstone and Brands Hatch, Moss achieved top results with victories further embellished by pole positions and new lap records. For the Tourist Trophy race at Goodwood, four 250 SWBs and three Aston DB4GTs were the principle

contenders in class. Tyre wear was of major significance with Moss bursting a worn one and going off during practice. In the event, Moss's three stops for tyres against the four of Parkes (250 SWB) and Salvadori (DB4GT), coupled with immaculate driving, won him the race. This seventh TT victory had a bonus prize in the shape of a birthday cake with seven candles presented by the Duchess of Richmond and Gordon.

Moss's final race in 2375 was in the Tourist Trophy at Nassau, where the untypical high wind and rain that prevailed, had no effect on the typical outcome of Moss setting fastest practice time and winning the race.

AUSTIN HEALEY
SEBRING SPRITE

Purchased new in 1961 by Cyril Simpson, S221 was a renowned member of Team 221 – other members, H221 and X221 being owned by David Harris and John Sprinzel respectively. Simpson made his car available for the Sebring 4-hour race and it was entered for Moss and Paul Hawkins to drive. In practice though, a slipping clutch decided Moss to drive PMO 200 instead and his sister, Pat Moss, partnered Hawkins for the race, to finish 7th. Returning for 1962, the race was reduced to three hours and described by the press as a case of 'what might have been'. Heavy rain allowed Moss's sheer driving ability to decimate the faster Abarths and the lead gained may have been enough to win as the track dried. However, a late pit stop for fuel to satisfy a spluttering engine let the Abarths pass and Moss finished 3rd.

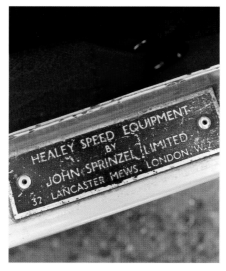

PORSCHE RS61

In the 1961 Targa Florio, the 2 litre RS60 finished second and third, but sadly, not first. Partnered with Graham Hill in a works car, Moss's hard won minute plus lead, evaporated when the differential let go on the final lap. A month later, the same drivers were invited to drive a 1.7 litre RS61 at the Nurburgring 1000 km race. Having uniquely started with rain tyres, lap times increased as the track dried, but when later it began to rain again, and then snow, their advantage returned as the leading Ferrari and others slowed. Moss, if anything, went faster and his placing rose from fifth to second. Hopes were high amongst the Moss supporters as he was about to overtake the leading Ferrari, but mechanical failure intervened and with it came the bitter disappointment of retirement.

Not ones to sit idly on the pit wall, Moss and Hill took over a Carrera Coupé and passed the Graham Martyn Lotus to win the 2 litre class.

SUNBEAM ALPINE

The Alpine name, previously used for 1953/54 Rally Cars was revived for the new sports car model of 1959, which was aimed principally at the American market. While Moss was driving a Lotus 19 sports car at the 1961 Riverside meeting, the Rootes competition manager, Ian Garrard, saw the chance of a little advertising and arranged for Moss and Brabham to drive a Sunbeam Alpine each in the 3 hour production car race. In practice, Moss's pale blue car suffered terminal engine problems, so for the race, Garrard arranged that Moss would share Brabham's car, nicknamed 'Rosebud'. Fortunately, somewhat improved publicity was the outcome of this plan with a class win and 3rd place overall.

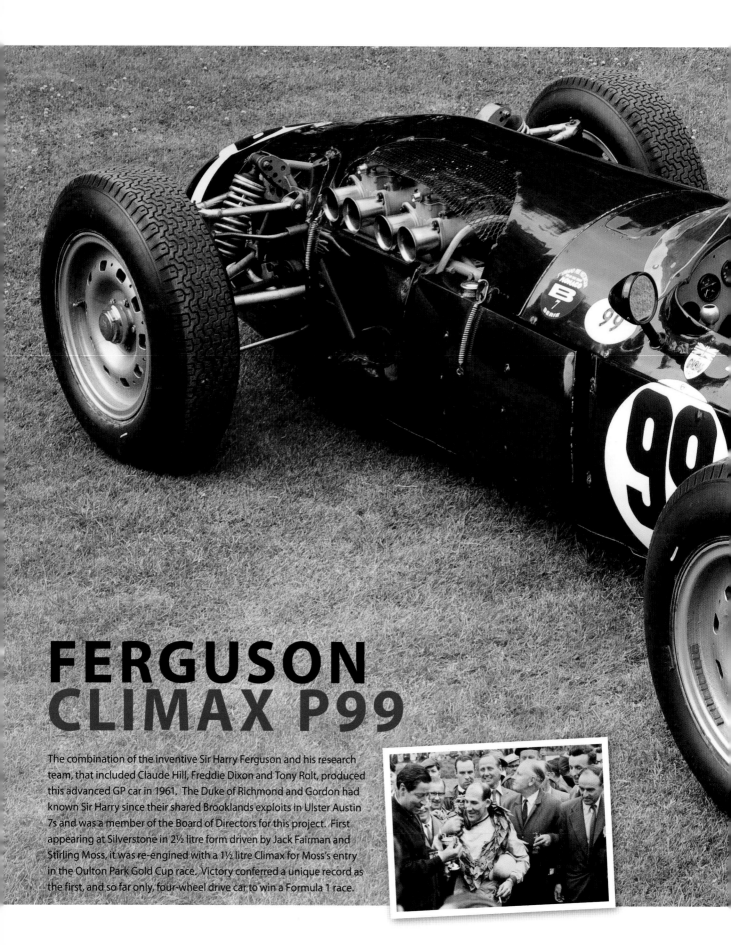

FERGUSON
CLIMAX P99

The combination of the inventive Sir Harry Ferguson and his research team, that included Claude Hill, Freddie Dixon and Tony Rolt, produced this advanced GP car in 1961. The Duke of Richmond and Gordon had known Sir Harry since their shared Brooklands exploits in Ulster Austin 7s and was a member of the Board of Directors for this project. First appearing at Silverstone in 2½ litre form driven by Jack Fairman and Stirling Moss, it was re-engined with a 1½ litre Climax for Moss's entry in the Oulton Park Gold Cup race. Victory conferred a unique record as the first, and so far only, four-wheel drive car to win a Formula 1 race.

SUPER SHELL

7

Ferguson

99

LOTUS 21

The Lotus 21 was a much lower, sleeker car than the 18, with its engine inclined to one side. At Monza in 1961, Moss was having trouble with the newly fitted engine on his 18/21 and looked unlikely to run. For fuel, the Rob Walker team was contracted to BP, and Lotus was with Esso, but an understanding was arrived at whereby Ireland offered his works Lotus 21 to Moss. Chassis 933 was prepared for Moss and raced with the unusual livery of Lotus green on the side panels and Walker blue on the top! Ferraris filled the first five grid places, with Moss starting 11th. Pretty rapidly,

the Ferrari assault was reduced to a lone Phil Hill, while Moss and Gurney had a tremendous battle for second place. This was resolved, not in Moss's favour, when on lap 36 he had to abandon the car with a collapsed wheel bearing. The new Rob Walker 21 then went to New Zealand for two further races, with Moss winning both. The first at Ardmore, was run in such bad weather that the race length was reduced; and the second at Christchurch, was so hot that a gamble to run on rain tyres only just paid off, with not even a trace of tread left at the end.

FERRARI 250 GTO

Certainly one of the Twentieth Century's most iconic motor cars, the GTO was conceived in 1961 as a racing development of the 250 SWB. It incorporated the potent 3 litre V12, Testa Rossa engine in the SWB chassis, all beautifully clothed under a lightweight body designed by Scaglietti.

Moss tested the prototype at Monza and was instantly impressed. Despite a total build number of 39 (homogolation required a minimum of 100), the cars were accepted for GT racing and made their race debut in March 1962, at the Sebring 12-hours. Four weeks later, in an arrangement with UDT, 3505 was delivered to Goodwood Motor Circuit, resplendent in the unique UDT-Laystall pale green livery. Entered for the Sussex Trophy at the Easter meeting on 23rd April 1962, Moss practiced the car in the company of Mike Parkes' similar GTO, 3589.

The Glover Trophy for Formula 1 cars preceded the Sussex Trophy and has passed into history as Stirling Moss's last race, following the accident at St. Mary's. On that day, 3505 sat silently, waiting to race another day.

KNIGHTS OF THE CIRCUITS

FROM MOTOR RACING, JUNE 1962

For the second time in two years, the people of Britain, almost as one, have been anxiously watching the recovery of Stirling Moss following a serious accident.

Disaster and tragedy strike frequently, often involving famous names. Yet few people would be capable of arousing the nation's emotions more than Stirling. It needs but little thought to appreciate the reason for this. Stirling lives dangerously, never fails to give of his best, and has become one of the symbols of our national pride.

He is an adventurer who, for fourteen years, has repeatedly brought prestige to his country, often against overwhelming odds. His record of international wins for Britain possibly exceeds that of any sportsman of any age; moreover, he has achieved this in one of the most hazardous spheres of human challenge.

Not all his successes have been on the circuit. His 'invisible earnings' have been reaped by the whole of Britain's motor industry. The country's thanks should surely be shown to one who has been such a wonderful ambassador.

That he hurt himself while giving the British public of his best, even when he had no hope of winning, has served only to strengthen the affection of the nation for a hero.

It is good to learn that Stirling is making steady progress, and we join with countless others in hoping that his recovery will be complete and that he will once again climb into the cockpit.

But whether or not he races again, let his achievements be acknowledged in a way that several other sporting celebrities have been honoured.

Let him join Henry Segrave, Malcolm Campbell, Jack Hobbs and Gordon Richards, for no one surely better deserves the accolade of knighthood.

The Birthday Honours will soon be announced. The name of Stirling Crauford Moss should rank high on that list.

HAPPIEST BIRTHDAY
GREAT FRIEND
QUEEN McLAU &
Ivan. 17·09·09.

'Yoppy
Birthday,
Stirling

Clive
and
Alison
Beecham

Happy Birthday
Vice-President!
Stuart Pringle
SECRETARY, SKOL

Parratt.